# The Dark
# Green Boots

## Kasia Reay

### Illustrated by Tania Rex

Schofield & Sims

It was summ<u>er</u>, but it kept r<u>ai</u>ni<u>ng</u>.
Gran t<u>oo</u>k Jo<u>sh</u> to get some b<u>oo</u>ts.

Some had tru<u>ck</u>s and some had st<u>ar</u>s, but the d<u>ar</u>k gr<u>ee</u>n b<u>oo</u>ts were the best fit.

The next morning it was still raining, but Josh went onto the deck.

A robin t<u>oo</u>k a drink next to him.
A <u>th</u>ru<u>sh</u> was l<u>oo</u>ki<u>ng</u> <u>for</u> slugs in
the wet s<u>oi</u>l.

Then Grandad took Josh along the cliffs. Some sand martins had nests in the rock.

There were some gu<u>ll</u>s in the <u>air</u>.
They were l<u>oo</u>ki<u>ng</u> d<u>ow</u>n to spot
f<u>oo</u>d on the sand <u>or</u> in the s<u>ur</u>f.

Then Josh and Grandad went down
the steep steps onto the sand.

Josh ran and his boots left clear footprints on the damp sand.

"Come and look! It's a rock pipit!"
said Grandad. He pointed to the rocks.

Then Josh went to look in the rockpools. He spotted a crab and three shrimps.

It had b<u>ee</u>n su<u>ch</u> a fun m<u>or</u>ni<u>ng</u>,
<u>th</u>anks to the d<u>ar</u>k gr<u>ee</u>n b<u>oo</u>ts!